Follow a Raindrop

by L.L. Owens

What You Already Know

Water is everywhere, and it is constantly changing form. Rain, snow, sleet, and hail are all forms of water. They are also called precipitation.

Evaporation is what happens when heat turns water into water vapor. Water vapor is an invisible gas found in the air. Depending on conditions, it can either remain invisible or be changed into visible water. Condensation is what happens when water vapor turns back into a liquid.

Most of the fresh water on Earth is frozen as ice. When rivers and lakes overflow, or when the ground can't take in any more water, wetlands form. You can also find groundwater, or fresh water, trapped below Earth's surface between underground rocks.

The water cycle keeps water moving. Water travels from Earth's surface into the air and back again. That's how we get the steady supply of fresh water we need to survive.

Water can be confusing to keep track of. After all, it takes many forms and is constantly changing. But without water, life could not exist. It is important that we know what's going on with Earth's water. This book will help you understand how water gets around our planet.

The Water of Life

Rain is a type of precipitation. It falls from the clouds to Earth's surface in the form of liquid droplets. Raindrops form when water vapor condenses around small particles of dust. When raindrops get too heavy for a cloud to hold them, they fall to the ground. Then we get wet!

Rain, if it falls too fast over too short a period of time, can cause many problems for humans and other living things. Heavy rain can make it difficult or unsafe to travel. It can even cause natural disasters such as mudslides and flooding. Yet most of the time, it is a lack of rain that causes the most harm to life on Earth.

Rain like this can cause heavy flooding, mudslides, and other serious problems.

All living things need water to survive. Rain is one way that many living things, such as plants and trees, get the water they need to live.

Rainwater helps supply the water that our bodies' systems run on. We drink it, water our crops with it, and cook with it. We also use it to wash our clothes, manufacture goods, and make electricity. For all of those reasons, the water that comes from rainfall is critical to maintaining life.

Evaporation

water evaporates

Evaporation is an important part of the water cycle. During the process of evaporation, water changes from a liquid state into a gas.

Here's how evaporation works. The Sun heats up water in rivers, lakes, and oceans. Once heated, the water turns into water vapor and rises into the atmosphere. All exposed areas of water, including swimming pools and reservoirs, are heated by the Sun and evaporate.

On warm, sunny days large amounts of water evaporate into the atmosphere.

Watery Planet

About 75 percent of Earth's surface is covered with water. Look at this view of Earth. Everything that is blue or white is some form of water!

Earth

Have you ever noticed steam rising from a cup of hot cocoa or a bowl of chicken soup? If you have, then you've seen evaporation with your own eyes. Steam is what water can look like before it turns to vapor and travels through the air.

A process called transpiration is another way water moves back into the air. Transpiration is what happens when plants release water into the air through their leaves. It's similar to the process of perspiration, when water leaves the human body as sweat and evaporates into the air.

Temperature plays a big role in evaporation. The hotter the water, whether it is found in a body of water or a living thing, the faster it will evaporate.

Condensation

clouds form

When water vapor cools in the air, it turns into tiny water droplets. The water has changed its form, or state, from a gas back into a liquid. This is a physical change called condensation.

A cloud is one visible result of condensation. Clouds form when water vapor condenses and turns to liquid high up in the atmosphere. When you look at a cloud, what you are really seeing is a large group of water droplets and ice crystals.

Now, think about the last time you had a glass of lemonade on a hot day. You might have noticed water droplets form on the outside of your glass. If you saw that happen, then you witnessed another example of condensation.

The water droplets that form on cold glasses of liquid come from the warm air. They begin as water vapor, which starts to cool down when it first touches the glass. Once it cools down enough, it changes state, or condenses, from a gas to a liquid.

Cloud Types

The three main types of clouds are cirrus, cumulus, and stratus. Have you seen them before?

cirrus clouds

cumulus clouds

stratus clouds

Rain

Rain falls.

Remember the water droplets that form clouds? When enough of them condense into large enough particles, they fall as rain. Clouds release the water droplets that they contain when the droplets become too heavy for the clouds to carry.

Meteorologists usually classify water droplets as rain when they reach a certain size. The diameter of a typical raindrop measures between one-half millimeter and four millimeters. Anything bigger than four millimeters is likely to break up into smaller drops.

Snow

In the United States, rain and snowfall are measured in inches. An equal measure of snow contains less water than rain. It can take fourteen inches of snow to equal the amount of water in one inch of rain!

Snow falling in the city

A rain shower contains raindrops of different sizes. Individual raindrops change size and shape as they fall. Such changes mostly happen when individual raindrops bump into each other while they are falling. Two raindrops might hit each other and form a bigger droplet. Or they might hit and break up into many smaller drops.

By using microscopes, scientists have been able to describe the shape of water droplets. Most raindrops start out in the shape of a sphere, but end up being shaped like a hamburger bun!

Back to the Sea

Water returns to the sea.

Rain feeds Earth's water systems. Those systems include rivers, lakes, streams, and oceans. Rivers, lakes, and streams are all connected through groundwater systems and the water cycle. Through evaporation, precipitation, and the movement of water, Earth's water systems constantly interact.

When a raindrop gets too heavy for a cloud to hold, it falls to Earth. That raindrop might fall into a river. It might land on top of a tree, splatter onto a flower, or drop to the ground. If you're outside, it might fall on you!

flowing river

Underground Water

Some water travels deep underground. When it reaches a layer of rock that it can no longer seep through, it can form underground lakes.

underground lake

Unless it lands in a body of water, a raindrop is likely to either evaporate back into the air, or be absorbed into the ground. Sometimes, the ground reaches its saturation point and cannot absorb any more water.

You can think of the ground as being like a sponge. When a sponge has been filled with too much water, the extra water spills out. When the ground reaches its saturation point, the extra water seeps out into streams, lakes, and wetlands.

From the streams, lakes, and wetlands, water flows to rivers. The water in rivers moves downstream toward the ocean. Water evaporates from the surface of the ocean and returns to the atmosphere.

The Complete Water Cycle

A single raindrop is just a tiny part of the water that moves through the water cycle. Earth's water is limited. But all of it moves through the water cycle, which is always active. The water cycle never stops changing water from one form to another or moving it from one place to another.

Heat from the Sun causes water to change form as it travels. When not in its liquid form, water travels as water vapor, or water that has evaporated. Water also travels in clouds as water droplets. It can also move from place to place as precipitation when it rains, snows, or hails.

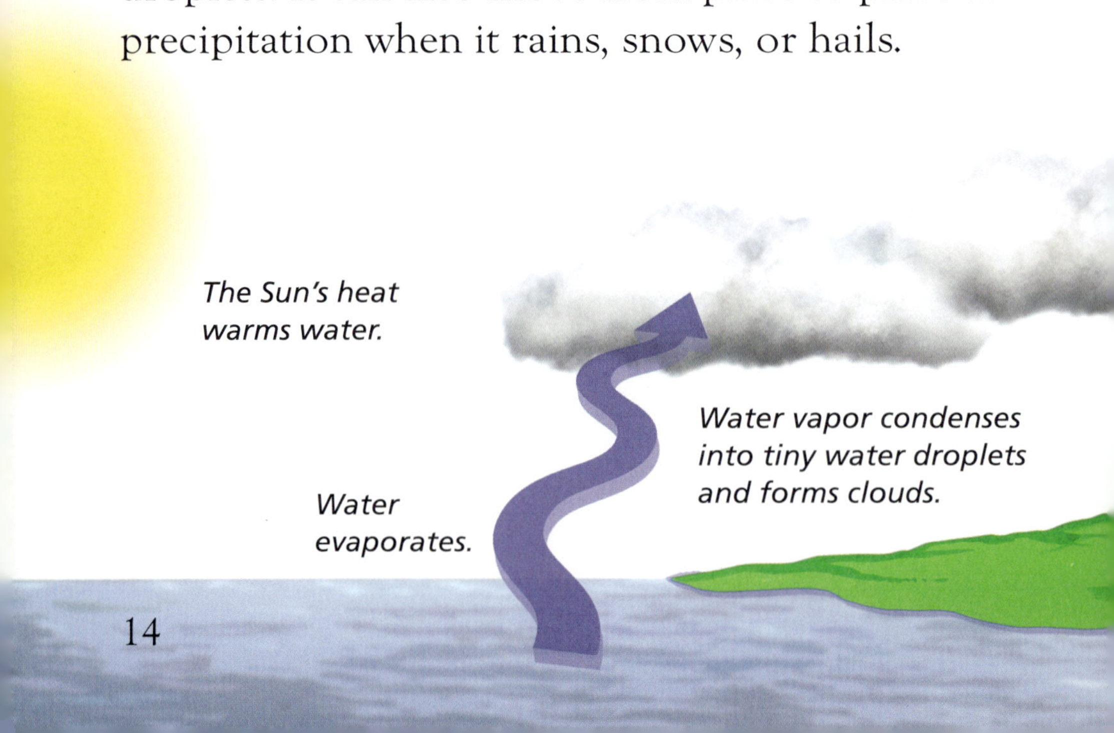

Everything on Earth is involved somehow in the water cycle. Plants and trees give off evaporated water that travels into the atmosphere. When we sweat, the water produced enters into the water cycle too.

Water reaches rivers, oceans, and lakes as precipitation and run-off. Soil absorbs water, which can trickle down to the rocks beneath the soil. Plants and trees can absorb some of that water to continue the cycle.

Much of the water cycle is visible. But other parts are invisible. For example, in the summer, single trees might evaporate hundreds of gallons of water a day!

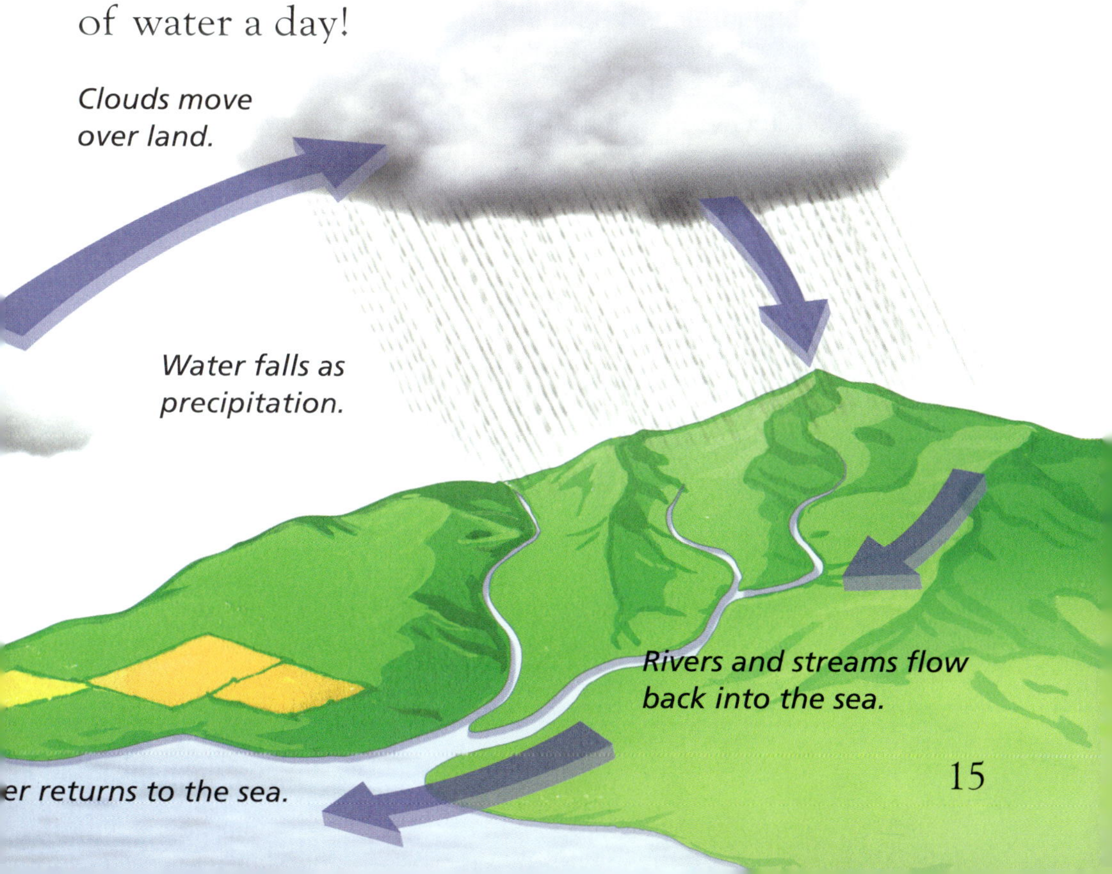

Glossary

atmosphere	the whole mass of air that surrounds Earth
classify	to assign something to a category
natural disaster	a natural event that happens suddenly and causes severe damage
perspiration	the process of perspiring, or sweating
saturation	being full of moisture
transpiration	the process of green plants giving off water through their leaves